MARVELLOUS MEETINGS

Marvellous Meetings

A Facilitator's Guide

Christine Newton

Gower

© Christine Newton 2001

The materials that appear in this book, other than those quoted from prior sources, may be reproduced for education/training activities. There is no requirement to obtain special permission for such uses.

This permission statement is limited to reproduction of materials for educational or training events. Systematic or large-scale reproduction or distribution – or inclusion of items in publications for sale – may be carried out only with prior written permission from the publisher.

Published by
Gower Publishing Limited
Gower House
Croft Road
Aldershot
Hants GU11 3HR
England

Gower Publishing Company
131 Main Street
Burlington VT 05401-5600 USA

Christine Newton has asserted her right under the Copyright, Designs and Patents Acts 1988 to be identified as the author of this book.

British Library Cataloguing in Publication Data

Newton, Christine
    Marvellous meetings: a facilitator's guide
    1.Business meetings
    I.Title
    658.4'56

ISBN 0 566 08423 6

Library of Congress Control number: 2001091701

Typeset in Palatino by Manton Typesetters, Louth, Lincolnshire and printed in Great Britain by TJ International Ltd, Padstow, Cornwall.

Contents

Making meetings work 1
Intervention strategies for the trainer or facilitator 5
Resources guide 19

Information Sheets 25
  1 Principles of effective meetings 27
  2 Documentation: The agenda 31
  3 Documentation: The minutes 36
  4 Documentation: The action plan 40

Check Lists 41
  1 Responsibilities of the Chair 43
  2 Responsibilities of the minute-taker 45
  3 Responsibilities of meetings attendees 47
  4 Jargon buster 49

Questionnaires 51
  1 How well am I doing as Chair? 52
  2 How well am I doing as minute-taker? 53
  3 How well am I doing at meetings? 54
  4 Jargon buster – How much do you know? 55

Work Sheets 59
  1 Running the meeting: communication skills for the Chair 61
  2 Managing behaviour: communication skills for the Chair 65

3	Constructive communication skills for meetings attendees	70
Cards		77
1	Running the meeting	79
2	Managing behaviour	83
3	Constructive and assertive communication skills	87
4	Bad behaviour at meetings	93
5	What would you do or say?	99
Appendices		113
1	Meeting intervention strategies	113
2	Assertive techniques	121
3	Some ideas on using the skill-building cards	123
4	Additional training themes	125

Making meetings work

A well-conducted meeting is one of the essential tools of effective management and good business practice. Yet how often have you heard, or expressed yourself, sentiments such as: 'I waste so much time at meetings. Last week we got through an hour's work – but it took us four hours to do it!'

It's not difficult to manage and conduct a successful meeting and this facilitator's guide, *Marvellous Meetings*, will give you the resources you need to affect the attitude, increase the knowledge and develop the skills of those who need to make meetings work.

Who

People who want to make meetings work, for example:

- Trainers and facilitators
- Existing Chairs
- Minute-takers
- Meetings attendees
- Managers
- Project team leaders
- Departmental or functional heads
- PTA members

- Social and church committee members
- New business entrepreneurs

Why

There are many benefits to be gained from making meetings work. Here are just a few:

- More efficient use of time
- Better decisions can be made
- Information can be shared efficiently
- Stress and frustrations are minimized
- Newcomers learn skills from observation
- Teams bond more successfully
- Interpersonal skills can be developed
- Communication skills can be developed
- The work gets done
- It's more fun and far more satisfying

What

Twenty-one resources that can be used in a variety of ways to build, or reinforce, the principles and skills necessary for making meetings work:

- Handouts
- Work sheets
- Questionnaires
- Activity cards
- Discussion cards
- Intervention strategies

How

Look at the *Marvellous Meetings* **Resources Guide** (pages 19–20). Decide on the areas you wish to improve or develop then choose the appropriate resources. If you need help in using these resources, look at the **Intervention Strategies for the Trainer or Facilitator**. Whether you're a project manager, a team leader, a committee member or any other interested party, you'll find many ideas to help you make your meetings work more effectively.

We've kept the theory of conducting meetings to a minimum. Most of us know the theory – it's the practical application of the theory that most of us need! That's what this 'tool kit' provides.

Intervention strategies for the trainer or facilitator

The following notes have been compiled to give you, the trainer or facilitator, a broad range of ideas for using these **Marvellous Meetings** resources. This list is by no means exhaustive. Our twenty-one resources are versatile and flexible, and we're sure that by the time you've looked through our list of hints and tips you will have come up with many other strategy and activity ideas of your own.

Resource List

- **Information Sheet 1:** Principles of effective meetings (pp 27–30)
- **Information Sheet 2:** Documentation – the agenda (pp 31–35)
- **Information Sheet 3:** Documentation – the minutes (pp 36–39)
- **Information Sheet 4:** Documentation – the action plan (p 40)

- **Check List 1:** Responsibilities of the Chair (pp 43–44)

- **Check List 2:** Responsibilities of the minute-taker (pp 45–46)
- **Check List 3:** Responsibilities of meetings attendees (pp 47–48)
- **Check List 4:** Jargon buster (pp 49–50)

- **Questionnaire 1:** How well am I doing as Chair? (p 52)
- **Questionnaire 2:** How well am I doing as minute-taker? (p 53)
- **Questionnaire 3:** How well am I doing at meetings? (p 54)
- **Questionnaire 4:** Jargon buster – How much do you know? (pp 55–57)

- **Work Sheet 1**: Running the meeting: communication skills for the Chair (pp 61–64)
- **Work Sheet 2:** Managing behaviour: communication skills for the Chair (pp 65–69)
- **Work Sheet 3:** Constructive communication skills for meetings attendees (pp 70–76)

- **Skill-building Cards for the Chair:** Running the meeting (pp 79–81)
- **Skill-building Cards for the Chair:** Managing behaviour (pp 83–85)
- **Skill-building Cards for Meetings Attendees:** Constructive and assertive communication skills (pp 87–91)
- **Skill-building Cards:** Bad behaviour at meetings (pp 93–97)

- **Discussion-generating Cards:** 'What would you do or say?' (pp 99–111)

- **Intervention Strategies** (pp 113–119)

Intervention strategies

1 Influencing others indirectly
   Raising awareness

If you need to raise awareness or pass training information to people who are senior to you or who are reluctant to put themselves on training courses you could send them copies of the following four information sheets for evaluation (though probably not all at once!).

Information Sheet 1: Principles of effective meetings
Information Sheet 2: Documentation – the agenda
Information Sheet 3: Documentation – the minutes
Information Sheet 4: Documentation – the action plan

While reading and evaluating the documents, they are absorbing the information.

An attached covering note should include some of the following points:

- We are considering using this new material for a forthcoming training workshop and would appreciate your feedback on the content.
- Do you think we match up to this level of quality/performance/expertise or do you think we fall short?
- Where do you think we fall short and what do you suggest we might do to improve our standards?
- What is your opinion of the agenda format? Should we change our own agenda format? Should we start using an agenda?
- What is your opinion of the minutes format? Should we change our minutes format? Should we start minuting our meetings?
- What is your opinion of the action plan? Should we start using one?

2   **Influencing others indirectly
    Raising awareness
    Personal skills audit**

Use the three check lists when you want the people you wish to influence to focus specifically on their own role.

**Check List 1: Responsibilities of the Chair
Check List 2: Responsibilities of the minute-taker
Check List 3: Responsibilities of meetings attendees**

As in strategy 1 above, an attached covering note should include some of the following notes:

- We are considering using this new material for a forthcoming training workshop and would appreciate your feedback on this description for your role as ....
- Do you think this is a fair description of your role?
- Would you make any changes to the description as it stands? If so, what do you suggest?
- Which part of this role do you find challenging – or did you find challenging when you were new and inexperienced?
- Can you give any hints and tips to others who might undertake this role in the future?

3   **Influencing others indirectly
    Raising awareness
    Personal skills audit**

If you have been able to use strategies 1 and 2 on the people you wish to influence indirectly, you might be able to encourage them to undertake a personal skills audit by using one of the three questionnaires:

**Questionnaire 1: How well am I doing as Chair?
Questionnaire 2: How well am I doing as minute-taker?
Questionnaire 3: How well am I doing at meetings?**

Ask the individual to comment on the document. Is it comprehensive? Will it make your trainees think more deeply about their own role? and so on, then invite the person to complete the questionnaire.

4. **Influencing others indirectly**
   Raising awareness
   Personal skills audit
   Giving feedback on performance
   Team building*

Following strategy 3, if the person you wish to influence is still open to the suggestion, you may be in a position to offer him or her feedback. The three questionnaires to use are:

Questionnaire 1: How well am I doing as Chair?
Questionnaire 2: How well am I doing as minute-taker?
Questionnaire 3: How well am I doing at meetings?

These can be given to all the members of a team, department or other meetings group in order to provide feedback on each other's performance.

It's useful to explain in a covering note the purpose of the feedback and that it may be given anonymously.

Once the forms have been completed, there are two options for collating and feeding back the results to the position holder:

1. Pass all the completed questionnaires to the person who is to receive the feedback.
2. Collate the information and produce a combined response sheet along the following lines:

---

* If the person you are trying to influence indirectly is open to receiving feedback from their team, department or meetings group, you may be able to take this forward into a **team-building** activity by bringing all relevant people together to discuss the findings. (You are now influencing directly!)

Knowledge	5	4	3	2	1
Keeping to the agenda	✓	✓✓	✓	✓	
Keeping attendees focused and to the point			✓✓	✓✓	✓

5 Training sessions at departmental or team meetings
Raising awareness
Personal skills audit
Giving feedback on performance
Team building

If you run regular departmental or team meetings and time is available, it is a useful practice to take some time, say 10 to 20 minutes, either at the beginning or the end of the meeting to deal with training issues. One of these issues might be to evaluate your meetings practice and improve your performance.

Each of the strategies 1 to 4 can be used equally successfully at departmental or team meetings training sessions.

Another advantage of conducting team sessions is that the process of evaluating your meetings becomes a team-building exercise in its own right.

Workshops

The following strategies are all described within the context of running training workshops. However, do remember that the flexibility and versatility of this set of resources means that an idea given in one strategy can easily be transposed into another.

Suggestions made for inclusion in a covering note, for example, (see strategies 1–4) can equally be made verbally in a departmental, team or other training session. Or, if your team is spread across the country and time cannot be allowed to evaluate your meetings practice when you do meet, then following strategies 1–4 can be useful here. However, within a team or departmental context, your influence will be direct and your requests for evaluation can be less subtle!

Included within each of the following strategies for running workshops are several ideas for conducting your training sessions. These are not intended to suggest that training 'must be done' this way but rather 'could be done' this way.

6 Training workshop
Raising awareness
Improving meetings practice

Use any combination of the information documents to generate discussion and debate in a training workshop.

Information Sheet 1: Principles of effective meetings
Information Sheet 2: Documentation – the agenda
Information Sheet 3: Documentation – the minutes
Information Sheet 4: Documentation – the action plan

Hold a round-table discussion with the whole training group
or
Break the larger group up into smaller syndicates, giving them a copy of the questions suggested below in printed form. Ask them to work separately and feedback their findings.

Questions to stimulate discussion and debate:

1. Do we agree with these six principles, or would we change this list?
   What would we add? What would we remove?
2. What does our company culture expect or tolerate?
3. Which meetings have we 'inherited'?
   Which meetings could be changed or removed entirely?
   What alternative business methods could we use?
4. Do we usually have the 'right people' at our meetings?
   Do we have the decision makers when we need them?
   Do we bring along the 'Assertive people' and leave the 'Passive and Aggressive people' behind?

Do we bring along the 'Adult' and leave the 'Parent' and 'Child' behind?
5. Do we always understand the purpose of our meetings?
Do we always understand the role we are expected to play at our meetings?
Do we play that role successfully?
6. Are our meetings well organized?
Where and how could we make improvements?
7. How skilled are we as individuals at our meetings?
Where do we need to improve?
8. How good are our meetings documents?
Where and how can we make improvements?
9. What changes can be made, within your authority, and who will be responsible for carrying out those changes?

7 Training workshop
Team building
Developing a professional code of conduct

This is a development of strategy 6 above, and uses the same information sheets:

Information Sheet 1: Principles of effective meetings
Information Sheet 2: Documentation – the agenda
Information Sheet 3: Documentation – the minutes
Information Sheet 4: Documentation – the action plan

Ask syndicates to work independently, assessing the current situation and deciding where improvements could be made.
From this initial activity, ask your syndicates to prepare a **Professional Code of Conduct** for all future meetings.
When you bring the groups together for feedback, give them the aim of combining their separate codes of conduct into one that can be agreed by all.
Discuss the viability of their Code of Conduct: how will it be introduced back at the workplace; who will be responsible for making sure that the Code of Conduct is adhered to?

8 Training workshop
Improving meetings documentation
Developing the skills of the minute-taker

Ask training participants to bring along existing documentation to compare and contrast with the examples given in the information sheets.

Information Sheet 2: Documentation – the agenda
Information Sheet 3: Documentation – the minutes
Information Sheet 4: Documentation – the action plan

Set the activity of rewriting their documents in the style suggested in the examples.

Prepare an agenda for a short meeting (10–20 minutes) to give the minute-taker the opportunity to take and produce a set of minutes.

Engage in discussion on how the new style might be introduced back at the workplace.

9 Training workshop
Jargon buster
Confidence building

This activity seeks to remove any feelings of intimidation (and as a result build confidence) that might arise by not knowing the jargon that is sometimes used at more formal meetings.

Check List 4: Jargon buster
Questionnaire 4: Jargon buster – how much do you know?

- Either start with the check list, clarify points through discussion and follow up with the questionnaire in the form of a game, quiz or competition to consolidate, or
- Start with the questionnaire in the form of a game, quiz or competition and use the check list to find the winner of the game.

10 Training workshop
Personal skills audit
Giving feedback on performance

Strategies 3 and 4 introduced the concept of a personal skills audit when influencing people indirectly. The same resources can be used during a training workshop.

Questionnaire 1: How well am I doing as Chair?
Questionnaire 2: How well am I doing as minute-taker?
Questionnaire 3: How well am I doing at meetings?

Individuals undertake the audit personally.
   Individuals take copies of the appropriate document and distribute them to those who would be able to give feedback on their performance at meetings.
   The trainer or facilitator can ensure anonymity by using the feedback process suggested in strategy 4.

11 Training workshop
Developing chairmanship skills in managing the meeting
Developing assertiveness

The Chair needs a particular set of skills that enables him or her to run and manage meetings effectively. The following two resources allow a range of activities to take place in a training workshop.

Work Sheet 1: Running the meeting: communication skills for the Chair
Skill-building Cards for the Chair: Running the meeting

Ask participants to explain how they currently run their meetings, the stages of their meetings, what they say at each stage and so on. Flipchart responses.
   Use the information printed on the left side of the work sheet to stimulate discussion and debate.
   Encourage participants to identify areas where they could improve their current performance.

Use the right side of the work sheet to record their own preferred wording at each stage of their meetings.

Prepare an agenda for a short meeting (10–20 minutes) and run a meeting for skill development.

Once participants are confident, use the cards as triggers.

Either,

- Ask the trainee Chair to select the trigger cards he or she wants to use, or
- You, the trainer, select and distribute the cards detailing the skills you wish to develop.

12 Training workshop
Developing chairmanship skills in managing behaviour
Developing assertiveness

The Chair needs a particular set of skills that enables him or her to manage the behaviour of the meetings attendees to ensure that the business of the meeting is conducted efficiently and effectively. The following three resources allow a range of activities to take place in a training workshop.

Work Sheet 2: Managing behaviour: communication skills for the Chair
Skill-building Cards for the Chair: Managing behaviour
Skill-building Cards: Bad behaviour at meetings

Ask participants to explain the current 'challenging' behaviours they face at meetings and how they deal with them. Flipchart responses.

Use the information printed on the left side of the work sheet to stimulate discussion and debate.

Encourage participants to identify areas where they could improve their current performance.

Use the right side of the work sheet to record their own preferred wording.

Set up practice sessions by dividing the group into twos or threes, and use the bad behaviour cards as triggers for 'bad behaviour' that needs to be dealt with assertively.

Prepare an agenda for a short meeting (10–20 minutes) and run a meeting for skill development.

Once participants are confident, use the skill-building cards as triggers. Either,

- Ask the trainee Chair to select the trigger cards he or she wants to use, or
- You, the trainer, select and distribute the cards detailing the skills you wish to develop.

Use the bad behaviour cards to provide triggers for the 'bad behaviour' during the meetings practice exercises.

13 Training workshop
Developing constructive communication skills for meetings attendees
Developing assertiveness

All meetings attendees need to practise constructive (and assertive) communications skills in order for a meeting to run efficiently and effectively. Develop these skills with:

Work Sheet 3: Constructive communication skills for meetings attendees
Skill-building Cards for Meetings Attendees: Constructive communication skills
Skill-building Cards: Bad behaviour at meetings

Ask participants to explain the current 'challenging' behaviours they face at meetings and how they deal with them. Flipchart responses.

Use the information printed on the left side of the work sheet to stimulate discussion and debate.

There are 20 assertive techniques listed in this resource. Each technique can be developed into a separate activity in its own right by giving examples, or asking participants to give examples, of other uses of this technique. (Details of assertive techniques are listed in Appendix 2, pp 121–122).

Encourage participants to identify areas where they could improve their current performance.

Use the right side of the work sheet to record their own preferred wording for dealing with the given situations.

Set up practice sessions by dividing group into twos or threes, and using the bad behaviour cards as triggers for 'bad behaviour' that needs to be dealt with assertively.

Prepare an agenda for a short meeting (10-20 minutes) and run a meeting for skill development.

Once participants are confident, use the skill-building cards as triggers. Either,

- Ask everyone to select the trigger cards he or she wants to use, or
- You, the trainer, select and distribute the cards detailing the skills you wish to develop.

Use the bad behaviour cards to provide triggers for the 'bad behaviour' during the meetings practice exercises.

14 Discussion and debate
Panel game or competition
Personal exploration
Presentation skills
Team building

One of the simplest, yet most effective, training methods is to gather a group of people around a table and engage in discussion and debate. The discussion-generating cards encourage and facilitate discussion and debate on all aspects of *Marvellous Meetings*.

Discussion-generating Cards: What would you do or say?

These address all the aspects of meetings that have already been covered in the previous 19 resources, so they work well in two ways:

1. As consolidation of work already covered.
2. As an alternative to the practical side of skills development, when time is short or training workshops

are not the right vehicle. For example, one or two *What would you do or say?* cards can be produced during a weekly team meeting in an ongoing effort to improve meetings skills. This also becomes another team-building activity.

The cards also lend themselves to a range of activities:

- Round-table discussion.
- Syndicate challenge – syndicates select cards and challenge each other.
- Panel game or competition.
- Pairing off. Pairs are given one or a selection of the cards and given time to prepare a strategy which they then present to the rest of the group.

In addition, these cards can act as triggers for:

- Reviewing assertive responses.
- Preparing a **Professional Code of Conduct**.
- Improving the performance of departmental teams when conducting their meetings.

Resources guide

The Chair

Raising understanding and awareness

- **Information Sheet 1:** Principles of effective meetings

Personal audit of current practice

- **Check List 1:** Responsibilities of the Chair
- **Questionnaire 1:** How well am I doing as Chair?

Feedback on current practice

- **Questionnaire 1:** How well am I doing as Chair?

Managing meetings – organizational skills

- **Information Sheet 2:** Documentation – the agenda
- **Information Sheet 3:** Documentation – the minutes
- **Information Sheet 4:** Documentation – the action plan
- **Work Sheet 1:** Running the meeting: communication skills for the Chair
- **Skill-building Cards for the Chair:** Running the meeting

Jargon busting

- **Check List 4:** Jargon buster
- **Questionnaire 4:** Jargon buster – how much do you know?

Managing behaviour at meetings

Work Sheet 2: Managing behaviour: communication skills for the Chair
Skill-building Cards for the Chair: Managing behaviour

Meetings attendees

Raising understanding and awareness
- **Information Sheet 1:** Principles of effective meetings

Personal audit of current practice
- **Check List 3:** Responsibilities of meetings attendees
- **Questionnaire 3:** How well am I doing at meetings?

Feedback on current practice
- **Questionnaire 3:** How well am I doing at meetings?

Managing at meetings
- **Information Sheet 2:** Documentation – the agenda
- **Information Sheet 3:** Documentation – the minutes
- **Information Sheet 4:** Documentation – the action plan

Jargon busting
- **Check List 4:** Jargon buster
- **Questionnaire 4:** Jargon buster – How much do you know?

Communicating at meetings
- **Work Sheet 3:** Constructive communication skills for meetings attendees
- **Skill-building Cards for Meetings Attendees:** Constructive communication skills

The minute-taker

Raising understanding and awareness
- **Information Sheet 1:** Principles of effective meetings

Personal audit of current practice
- **Check List 2:** Responsibilities of the minute-taker
- **Questionnaire 2:** How well am I doing as minute-taker?

Feedback on current practice
- **Questionnaire 2:** How well am I doing as minute-taker?

Managing at meetings
- **Information Sheet 2:** Documentation – the agenda
- **Information Sheet 3:** Documentation – the minutes
- **Information Sheet 4:** Documentation – the action plan

Jargon busting
- **Check List 4:** Jargon buster
- **Questionnaire 4:** Jargon buster – How much do you know?

Communicating at meetings
- **Work Sheet 3:** Constructive communication skills for meetings attendees
- **Skill-building Cards for Meetings Attendees:** Constructive communication skills

The trainer/facilitator

Resource List

- **Information Sheet 1:** Principles of effective meetings
- **Information Sheet 2:** Documentation – the agenda
- **Information Sheet 3:** Documentation – the minutes
- **Information Sheet 4:** Documentation – the action plan

- **Check List 1:** Responsibilities of the Chair
- **Check List 2:** Responsibilities of the minute-taker
- **Check List 3:** Responsibilities of meetings attendees
- **Check List 4:** Jargon buster

- **Questionnaire 1:** How well am I doing as Chair?
- **Questionnaire 2:** How well am I doing as minute-taker?
- **Questionnaire 3:** How well am I doing at meetings?
- **Questionnaire 4:** Jargon buster – how much do you know?

- **Work Sheet 1:** Running the meeting: communication skills for the Chair
- **Work Sheet 2:** Managing behaviour: communication skills for the Chair
- **Work Sheet 3:** Constructive communication skills for meetings attendees

- **Skill-building Cards for the Chair:** Running the meeting
- **Skill-building Cards for the Chair:** Managing behaviour
- **Skill-building Cards for Meetings Attendees:** Constructive communication skills
- **Skill-building Cards:** Bad behaviour at meetings

- **Discussion-generating Cards:** 'What would you do or say?'

- **Intervention Strategies**

See also the preceding section, Intervention strategies for the trainer/facilitator.

Information Sheets

1 Principles of effective meetings

2 Documentation – the agenda

3 Documentation – the minutes

4 Documentation – the action plan

Principles of effective meetings

Information Sheet 1

1. **ORGANIZATIONAL CULTURE expects meetings to be conducted effectively and does not tolerate ineffective behaviours.**

    In some organizations, unpunctuality, lack of preparation, rambling presentations, not focusing on the point under discussion, critical or cynical questioning, even not participating at all, is not only tolerated, but accepted as normal behaviour.

    In other organizations, arriving late for a meeting or being unprepared would not be a consideration. Expectations are high; everyone is prepared; presentations and discussions are to the point and professionally conducted.

    The two examples above show how organizational culture is reflected in meetings behaviour.

    Expectations are set – by the culture – then behaviour matches expectations.

2. **Meetings are APPROPRIATE for the outcome required.**

    An effective meeting is one in which the business under discussion could not be conducted more efficiently through some other medium (for example, letter, memo, e-mail or telephone).

    Inappropriate meetings are those that have been 'inherited' or continue through habit: *'We've always done it this way'; 'That's how this organization has always conducted its business'*.

3. **The 'RIGHT' PEOPLE attend the meeting.**

    - The right number of people are in attendance – not too many so that discussions become unwieldy; not too few so that business cannot be progressed.
    - Everyone in attendance has a contribution to make that they could not have made in a more appropriate way.
    - If decisions have to be reached, the decision-makers are there.

27

Reproduced from *Marvellous Meetings*,
Christine Newton, Gower, Aldershot

Principles of effective meetings

Information Sheet 1 continued

- If the meeting is long, the business is organized and timetabled so that individual contributors are able to attend when needed and leave when appropriate to do so.
- In behavioural terms, the aggressive and passive elements of our personalities are left behind while the assertive, professional 'person' attends.
- In transactional analysis* terms, the Parent and Child in each of us is left behind while the Adult person attends.

  * If transactional analysis is new to you, read *Transactional Analysis Today* by Ian Steward and Vann Joines, Lifespace, reprinted 1996

4. **Everyone understands the PURPOSE of the meeting and the ROLE they are expected to play.**

   Meetings are held for many reasons, which include:

   - Statutory requirement
   - Exchange of information
   - Decision making
   - Problem solving
   - Team working
   - Project management
   - Co-ordinating business functions
   - Planning, organizing, controlling
   - Reporting back
   - Committee work

   Whatever the reason, it's essential that the purpose of the meeting is understood by everyone attending, together with the role they are expected to play.

   - **The Team Leader** or Chair knows how to run the meeting effectively and focus attention on the purpose of the meeting. (see Check List 1: Responsibilities of the Chair).
   - **The major contributors** know how to present their case or their information precisely, concisely and keep

Reproduced from *Marvellous Meetings*,
Christine Newton, Gower, Aldershot

Principles of effective meetings

Information Sheet 1 continued

to the point. They also know how to build commitment, sell an idea and deal with negativity (see Work Sheet 3: Constructive communication skills for meetings attendees).

- **Those in attendance** know how to listen and reflect; ask pertinent questions that move the business along; ask for clarification when they need it; know how to disagree or contradict constructively (see Work Sheet 3: Constructive communication skills for meetings attendees).
- The level of formality/informality is appropriate to the type of meeting.

5. **The meetings are WELL ORGANIZED and PROPERLY DOCUMENTED.**

- An appropriate amount of notice is given.
- The **agenda** has been constructed appropriately (see Information Sheet 2: Documentation – the agenda).
- The **minutes** are drafted, agreed and circulated while the thoughts and memories are still fresh in the participants' minds (see Information Sheet 3: Documentation – the minutes).

6. **The Individuals have APPROPRIATE INTERPERSONAL AND COMMUNICATIONS SKILLS** (see Work Sheet 3: Constructive communication skills for meetings attendees).

The basic interpersonal and communication behaviours required of all effective meetings participants include how to:

- Present a business case, an idea, or information.
- Persuade and influence others – negotiate.
- Ask questions non-aggressively.
- Disagree non-judgementally.
- Clarify understanding.
- Keep oneself and others to the point.
- Manage time.
- Encourage others to make their contributions.

Reproduced from *Marvellous Meetings*,
Christine Newton, Gower, Aldershot

Principles of effective meetings

Information Sheet 1 concluded

- Deal with other people's inappropriate behaviour.

In addition, the Chair must also display the appropriate interpersonal and communications skills that enable him or her to conduct the meeting effectively (see Work Sheet 1: Running the meeting: communication skills of the Chair) and manage the behaviour of others (see Work Sheet 2: Managing behaviour: communication skills for the Chair).

Principles of effective meetings in a 'nutshell'

1. ORGANIZATIONAL CULTURE expectations
2. Meetings are APPROPRIATE
3. The 'RIGHT' PEOPLE attend
4. Everyone understands the PURPOSE and their ROLE
5. WELL ORGANIZED and PROPERLY DOCUMENTED
6. Appropriate INTERPERSONAL and COMMUNICATIONS SKILLS

Reproduced from *Marvellous Meetings*,
Christine Newton, Gower, Aldershot

Documentation – the agenda

Information Sheet 2

In meetings that work,

- The agenda has been constructed to state:
  - the topic under discussion
  - the objective of the discussion
  - the time allocated to that discussion

---

5. CO-OPTED GOVERNORS   **15 minutes**

To review current membership and list people to be co-opted together with reasons for their co-option.

- The agenda does not contain too many items. A realistic assessment has been made about the amount of business that can be conducted in the allocated period of time.
- The timing of agenda items has been realistically calculated.
- The agenda is well constructed, in the right order, and aids the running of the meeting (see example below of a formal agenda).

Matters arising

If the meetings organizer can find out ahead of time what items are likely to be raised under 'matters arising from the previous meeting', these can be listed to prevent surprises. Attendees can also be asked to consider these points before attending the meeting, which will lead to a better-informed level of debate.

Circulating documents before the meeting

Documents are circulated before the meeting with the expectation (see previous point on company culture) that they will be read and considered beforehand. This contributes to the effective use of meeting time and leads to a better-informed level of debate.

Reproduced from *Marvellous Meetings*,
Christine Newton, Gower, Aldershot

Documentation – the agenda

Information Sheet 2 continued

'Any other business'

Including this item is no longer considered to be effective business meetings practice. It encourages the tactical player to introduce surprise items and invites ill-prepared discussion on topics that can range from the irrelevant to the extremely important. If an item is irrelevant, it should not be raised. If an item is important, it should be raised as an agenda item.

Reproduced from *Marvellous Meetings*,
Christine Newton, Gower, Aldershot

Documentation – the agenda

Information Sheet 2 continued

A Formal Agenda

**ELMTREES MIDDLE SCHOOL
GOVERNORS' MEETING
to be held in the Staff Room on
Wednesday, 24 September 200*, 7.00 pm – 9.00 pm**

AGENDA

1. **ELECT CHAIRMAN, VICE CHAIRMAN** *(if not already appointed)*

2. **APOLOGIES FOR ABSENCE**

3. **MINUTES OF THE LAST MEETING**

    To be agreed and accepted or amended as appropriate.

4. **MATTERS ARISING FROM PREVIOUS MINUTES**

5. **CO-OPTED GOVERNORS**   15 minutes

    To review current membership and list people to be co-opted together with reasons for their co-option.

6. **OFSTED ACTION PLAN**   30 minutes

    To discuss inspector's report and draft action plans for submission next term.

7. **POLICIES AND PROCEDURES**   30 minutes

    To consider the issuing of guidelines for policy setting. To review existing policies and consider changes.

8. **DATE AND TIME OF NEXT MEETING**

Reproduced from *Marvellous Meetings*,
Christine Newton, Gower, Aldershot

Documentation – the agenda

Information Sheet 2 continued

Agenda for a routine (team or project) meeting

This example shows how a statement of purpose, a statement of outcomes and a list of the documents to be read before the meeting can also be used to focus attention.

Purchasing Team Meeting

Date:	14 April	**Location:**	Meeting Room G1
Start:	9.30 am (prompt)	**Finish:**	10.45 am

Attendees: CN (leading); GB; CD; RHa; RHi; JP; SW

Purpose: To update the team on project XYZ and agree new code of conduct for future purchasing contracts.

Outcome: First draft of new purchasing code of conduct.

Documents: Minutes of last meeting; current code of conduct – **to be read before the meeting**.

AGENDA

1.	Review of progress on actions agreed at last meeting	GB	10 mins
		RHi	10 mins
2.	Report on progress of project XYZ	SW	10 mins
3.	New code of conduct for future purchasing contracts	All	30 mins
4.	Next steps	All	5 mins
5.	Next meeting	All	5 mins

Reproduced from *Marvellous Meetings*,
Christine Newton, Gower, Aldershot

Documentation – the agenda

Information Sheet 2 concluded

Unscheduled meetings

When an unscheduled meeting is required – for example an essential team briefing, crisis limitation or where an on-the-spot-decision is needed – the principles listed above still apply, albeit in an informal way. The purpose of the meeting is stated; the need is clarified; the point of discussion is focused.

The 'back-of-an-envelope' agenda

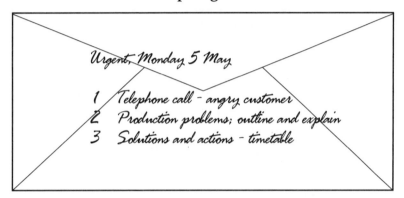

Reproduced from *Marvellous Meetings*,
Christine Newton, Gower, Aldershot

Documentation – the minutes

Information Sheet 3

Once the meeting has been completed, the **minutes** are drafted, agreed and circulated while the thoughts and memories are still fresh in the participants' minds.

The minutes of a meeting form the official record of events. Subject to any comments or amendments at the next meeting, the Chair will sign the minutes as 'being a correct record'.

Minutes are an essential document for several reasons:

- To inform absent members of the events of the meeting.
- To identify decisions and actions to be taken as a result of discussion and agreement.
- To ensure that the decisions and actions have been carried through.
- To aid decision-making at a later date.
- The minutes of a democratically elected body may also serve to show constituents what elected members are doing on their behalf.
- In exceptional circumstances, minutes have been presented in a court of law.

Minutes do not have to be lengthy or complicated but they should cover the following key points:

- Time, date and place of the meeting.
- Names of those present and any apologies for absence.
- All items discussed, together with conclusions reached, decisions made and actions agreed.
- Names of those responsible for actions to be taken.
- *In some cases* the main arguments or steps leading to decisions.
- The date, time and location of the next meeting.

> **The specific layout, style and content of minutes** are governed by the rules that regulate committee procedure, or conform to tradition or house style.

Reproduced from *Marvellous Meetings*,
Christine Newton, Gower, Aldershot

Documentation – the minutes

Information Sheet 3 continued

The language of minutes

Minutes are usually written in indirect or reported speech. For example:

Direct speech: *'So we're all agreed then. We're going to follow plan A.'*

Reported speech: *It was unanimously agreed that plan A would be followed.*

Modern practice

- Use 'mind mapping' as a minute-taking tool.
- Use a flipchart to bullet point contributions and action points, then use the flipchart notes as the basis of the minutes.
- Write up simple action minutes to include:
    - What actions were agreed.
    - Who is responsible.
    - Dates and deadlines.

Reproduced from *Marvellous Meetings*, Christine Newton, Gower, Aldershot

Documentation – the minutes
Information Sheet 3 continued

A set of minutes for a social club committee meeting – reported speech

THE RAQUETTES SQUASH CLUB

Meeting No 123

Minutes of the General Committee Meeting of The Raquettes Squash Club held in the Club House at 1930 hrs on Monday 24 April 200-.

Present: Miss P Andrews (in the Chair)
Mr N Marston (Hon Sec)
Mrs A Hopwood (Treasurer)
Miss T Turning
Mr B Wills
Mr T Thomas
Mr J Thompson

Apologies: An apology was received from Mrs P Yelland.

Minutes: The minutes of the meeting held on 22 March 200-, having been circulated to the members, were taken as read and approved and signed by the Chair.

Matters arising: Miss Turning reported that as a result of an advertisement in the local evening newspaper and the efforts of the playing members in particular, eight new players had joined the club.

Mr Wills and Mr Thomas presented a memorandum showing their proposals. After considerable discussion it was unanimously agreed to accept the proposals in full. A vote of thanks was proposed by Mr Thompson and seconded by Mrs Hopwood.

Secretary's report: Mr Marston reported that he had received a letter of complaint from one of the members, Miss C Manhatten, about the state of the Club House. After a statement from the Chair it was agreed to leave the matter on the table. The secretary was instructed to acknowledge receipt of the complaint.

Treasurer's report: Mrs Hopwood circulated a statement showing the current financial position. She pointed out that the rates were due to be paid and that there was an electricity bill outstanding.

Purchase of a new notice board: The Chair reported that following a conversation with several members about the condition of the old notice board, most of them felt it was now inadequate. It was agreed to purchase a new one.

Next meeting: It was agreed to hold the next meeting on 21 May 200* at 1930 hrs in the Club House.

Chair

25 April 200*

Reproduced from *Marvellous Meetings*,
Christine Newton, Gower, Aldershot

Documentation – the minutes

Information Sheet 3 concluded

Action minutes for a routine (team or project) meeting

MINUTES of the Design Progress Meeting

Date: 1 February   **Location:** Meeting Room 204

Attendees: PA (leading); AM; NM; TO; VP; SC; CS

Apologies: EF

1. *Review of last meeting:*

    NM reported that site visits had increased by 15%.
    TO brought the matter of health and safety violations to the group's attention.

2. *Progress report on project ABC:*

    SR reported that progress on the ABC project was below expectations. As a result it was agreed that:

    PA would *xxx*
    AM would *yyy*
    SR would zzz

3. *Replacement supplier:*
    It was unanimously agreed that the replacement supplier for … would be …

    CS to pursue the contract.

4. *Next meeting:* 2 March

PA
3 February

Reproduced from *Marvellous Meetings*,
Christine Newton, Gower, Aldershot

Documentation – the action plan

Information Sheet 4

In addition to the actions listed within the minutes, a separate **action plan** can also be useful in bringing agreed actions to everyone's attention – and especially to the attention of those who have agreed to undertake them.

This action plan becomes a useful organizing and controlling tool at subsequent meetings.

Action plan

<u>**THE RAQUETTES SQUASH CLUB – ACTION PLAN
from Monday 24 April 200***</u>

	Action	Member	Date agreed/ completed
1	Progress proposal.	Bruce and Tom	
2	Acknowledge letter of complaint.	Nigel	
3	Pay rates and electricity bills.	Antony	
4	Purchase new notice board.	Tom	

Reproduced from *Marvellous Meetings*,
Christine Newton, Gower, Aldershot

Check Lists

1 Responsibilities of the Chair

2 Responsibilities of the minute-taker

3 Responsibilities of meetings attendees

4 Jargon buster

Responsibilities of the Chair

Check List 1

The responsibility for ensuring that meetings are competently managed and professionally conducted lies squarely on the shoulders of the person chairing the meeting. The Chair's knowledge of the role, leadership styles and interpersonal skills all play a part here and can include:

Knowledge

- Standing orders; committee procedure
- Meetings procedures and etiquette
- History of decisions made
- Background of meeting participants; for example, skills and expertise
- Behavioural styles (and how to 'manage' them)

Skills

- Agreeing the draft agenda
- Insisting on prompt attendance
- Welcoming and introducing new members
- Dealing with matters of procedure in either formal or non-formal meetings
- Stating, or clarifying, the point and purpose of the meeting
- Initiating discussion on the agenda items
- Keeping to the agenda
- Keeping attendees focused and to the point
- Ensuring relevance of discussions
- Dealing with 'hidden agendas' (that is, unstated personal objectives)
- Dealing with inappropriate behaviours: negativity, cynicism, aggression, etc.
- Dealing with unskilled behaviours: waffling presentations; nervousness, etc.
- Controlling the over-talkative
- Challenging generalizations, subjective statements, exaggerations, assumptions, etc.
- Encouraging the quieter members to participate
- Giving acknowledgements and thanks for contributions
- Clarifying and summarizing points

Reproduced from *Marvellous Meetings*, Christine Newton, Gower, Aldershot

Responsibilities of the Chair

Check List 1 concluded

- Moving the discussion towards a decision or taking a vote
- Managing the time
- Ensuring that all essential business is dealt with
- Agreeing follow-up actions and the draft minutes; allocating the organizational tasks
- Taking any personal follow-up action and monitoring the follow-up action of others

Attitude

- Confident and professional
- Assertive and open-minded
- Thorough but organized and time-conscious
- Friendly, approachable, encouraging
- Diplomatic and supportive
- A 'completer-finisher' – gets things done.

Reproduced from *Marvellous Meetings*,
Christine Newton, Gower, Aldershot

Responsibilities of the minute-taker

Check List 2

The minutes of a meeting are important as they are an official record of the business undertaken at a meeting: discussions, individual contributions, votes taken, decisions reached, actions agreed and so on. An official copy of each set of minutes, bearing the Chair's signature, should be kept for reference. A set of minutes should be able to stand up in a court of law.

The style of minutes varies considerably and can range from a full verbatim report (which is not common) to a brief set of notes or 'bullet points'. The style chosen will be influenced by company or house styles, the past practice of previous job-holders or the preferences of the current manager. Generally, reported speech is used.

The minute-taker's knowledge of the role, skills and attitudes can include:

Knowledge

- Standing orders
- Committee procedure
- Meetings procedures and etiquette
- Type and style of minutes needed
- History of decisions made
- How to interact with the Chair

Skills

- Taking responsibility for accurately recording the main points of the discussion, decisions taken and actions agreed at the meeting
- Liaising with the Chair to agree type and style of minutes needed
- Liaising with the Chair to agree content and phrasing of minutes – asking for clarification during the meeting as required
- Recording members attending and apologies for absence
- Correctly attributing contributions as appropriate
- Assisting with organizational requirements
- Assisting with time-keeping

Reproduced from *Marvellous Meetings*,
Christine Newton, Gower, Aldershot

Responsibilities of the minute-taker

Check List 2 concluded

- Producing draft minutes for the Chair's approval
- Producing and distributing final minutes within an agreed time scale
- Ensuring that minute-taking is his/her prime function at the meeting. If the minute-taker wishes to make a contribution on any point, the task of minute-taking should be passed on to someone else (perhaps the Chair)

Attitudes

- Accurate
- Thorough and organized
- Time-conscious
- Confident and professional
- Diplomatic
- Assertive

Reproduced from *Marvellous Meetings*,
Christine Newton, Gower, Aldershot

Responsibilities of meetings attendees

Check List 3

If a meeting is to be successful then *everyone* must take some degree of ownership and responsibility. The amount of ownership and responsibility taken by the meetings attendees will, to some extent, be regulated by the organization's culture, but much, of course, also depends on the individual's disposition.

Meeting attendees should consider the following:

Knowledge

- Meetings procedures and etiquette
- Different behavioural styles (and how to interact with them)
- Presentation and public speaking techniques
- General communication techniques

Skills

- Punctuality
- Preparation:
  - Reads all appropriate papers before the meeting
  - Prepares thoughts (or makes notes) on topics for discussion
  - Prepares notes on their own presentation topics
- Informs the Chair if unable to attend
- Informs the Chair of time constraints – that is, when they can attend; when they'd like to speak; when they need to leave
- Keeps to the agenda item
- Keeps focused on the topic under discussion
- Listens without interrupting
- Speaks confidently on their own topics
- Makes a contribution to other people's topics
- Asks questions in a non-aggressive way
- Respects different opinions
- Disagrees constructively
- Engages in debate
- Helps in the decision-making process

Reproduced from *Marvellous Meetings*,
Christine Newton, Gower, Aldershot

Responsibilities of meetings attendees

Check List 3 concluded

Attitude

- Confident and professional
- Assertive
- Diplomatic
- Open-minded but decisive when appropriate
- Constructive, even when disagreeing

Reproduced from *Marvellous Meetings*,
Christine Newton, Gower, Aldershot

Jargon buster

Check List 4

Don't get confused if someone uses meetings jargon. Prepare yourself!

Term	Meaning
Abstention	Someone who does not vote for or against a motion.
Ad hoc committee	A committee formed to deal with a single unit of work. Once this work had been completed, the committee disbands.
Addendum	An addition or an alteration to a proposed motion.
Address the Chair	In some formal meetings, those who wish to speak must first address the chairman with 'Mr Chairman' or 'Madam Chairman'.
Adjournment	The proceedings are suspended and the meeting is reconvened at a later date to complete the unfinished business.
Annual General Meeting	A statutory meeting held once a year, open to an organization's whole membership.
Ballot	A written, secret vote.
Board meeting	A management meeting of a company's board of directors.
Casting vote	A second and deciding vote allowed to the chairman when the votes for and against a motion are equal.
Co-opted member	One invited to serve on a committee by the majority of existing members.
Ex officio member	One who attends a meeting 'by virtue of their office' but without voting rights, i.e. secretary to the committee.
Executive committee	A committee that undertakes the management of an organization.
Extraordinary General Meeting	A special meeting called to deal with an urgent problem or emergency situation.
in camera	In private – not open to the public.
intra vires	Within the legal power or authority of the organization.
Lie on the table	A motion is said to 'lie on the table' when it is decided to take no action upon it.
Memorandum and Articles of Association	Documents in which the structure and management of an organization are set out.
Motion	A formal proposal moved by a member that certain action be taken.

Reproduced from *Marvellous Meetings*,
Christine Newton, Gower, Aldershot

Jargon buster

Check List 4 concluded

Term	Meaning
Move the closure	This phrase is used to indicate the discussion should end and a vote taken.
nem con	No one contradicting, though some may have abstained from voting.
nem dis	No one dissenting.
Out of order	If a member is not keeping to the point under discussion or is speaking improperly he or she is said to be 'out of order'.
Point of order	A member can raise a 'point of order' during a meeting which is a query about a possible infringement of procedure.
Postponement	A meeting is held at a later date.
Proposer	One who puts forward a motion for discussion at a meeting.
Proxy vote	A vote taken on behalf of someone unable to attend a meeting.
Quorum	The minimum number of people who must attend to constitute a meeting. This number will be indicated in the Standing Orders.
Resolution	A motion passed by a majority vote becomes a resolution.
Rider	An addition to a resolution (already passed) which must also be voted for.
Seconder	One who supports the proposer of a motion before the vote is taken.
sine die	For an indefinite period.
Standing committee	A permanent committee carrying on day-to-day work.
Standing orders	The rules of an organization that regulate committee procedure.
Tabled	This describes a document that has not been circulated before a meeting but is presented at the meeting.
Teller	One appointed to count votes.
Terms of reference	A statement of the work to be carried out by the members of a committee.
ultra vires	Outside the legal power or authority of an organization.
Unanimous vote	All votes are for or against a motion.
Verbatim report	An exact or word-for-word report.

Reproduced from *Marvellous Meetings*,
Christine Newton, Gower, Aldershot

Questionnaires

1 How well am I doing as Chair?

2 How well am I doing as minute-taker?

3 How well am I doing at meetings?

4 Jargon buster – how much do you know?

How well am I doing as Chair?

Questionnaire 1

Use the following check list to gauge your skill at chairing meetings.

For real insight, give a copy of this check list to the people who attend the meetings you Chair and ask them for honest feedback.

Scale: **1 = needs work! 5 = excellent every time!** Use n/a wherever a section is not applicable to your role, in self assessments, and where you are unable to give feedback.

Knowledge	5	4	3	2	1
Standing orders; committee procedure					
Meetings procedures and etiquette					
History of decisions made					
Background of meeting participants i.e. skills and expertise					
Behavioural styles (and how to 'manage' them)					
Behaviours (skills)					
Agrees the draft agenda					
Insists on prompt attendance					
Welcomes and introduces new members					
Deals with matters of procedure in formal and non-formal meetings					
States, or clarifies, the point and purpose of the meeting					
Initiates discussion on the agenda items					
Keeps to the agenda					
Keeps attendees focused and to the point					
Ensures relevance of discussions					
Deals with 'hidden agendas' (i.e. unstated personal objectives)					
Deals with inappropriate behaviours: negativity, cynicism, aggression					
Deals with unskilled behaviour: waffling presentations; nervousness					
Controls the over-talkative					
Challenges generalizations, subjective statements, exaggerations, assumptions, etc.					
Encourages the quieter members to participate					
Gives acknowledgements and thanks for contributions					
Clarifies and summarizes points					
Moves the discussion towards a decision or taking a vote					
Manages the recording of the minutes					
Manages time					
Ensures that all essential business is dealt with					
Agrees follow-up actions and the draft minutes					
Allocates the organizational tasks					
Takes any personal follow-up action					
Monitors the follow-up action of others					
Attitude					
Confident and professional					
Assertive and open-minded					
Thorough but organized and time-conscious					
Friendly, approachable and encouraging					
Diplomatic and supportive					
A 'completer-finisher' – gets things done					

Reproduced from *Marvellous Meetings*,
Christine Newton, Gower, Aldershot

How well am I doing as minute-taker?

Questionnaire 2

Use the following check list to gauge your skill as minute-taker.

For real insight, give a copy of this check list to the people who attend the meetings at which you take minutes and ask them for honest feedback.

Scale: **1 = needs work! 5 = excellent every time!** Use n/a wherever a section is not applicable to your role, in self assessments, and where you are unable to give feedback.

Knowledge	5	4	3	2	1
Standing orders					
Committee procedure					
Meetings procedures and etiquette					
Type and style of minutes needed					
History of decisions made					
How to interact with the Chair					
Behaviours (skills)					
Agrees the draft agenda					
Takes responsibility for accurately recording the main points of the discussion, decisions taken and actions agreed at the meeting					
Liaises with the Chair to agree type and style of minutes needed					
Liaises with the Chair to agree content and phrasing of minutes					
Asks for clarification during the meeting as required					
Records members attending and apologies for absence					
Correctly attributes contributions as appropriate					
Assists with organizational requirements					
Assists with time-keeping					
Produces draft minutes for the Chair's approval					
Produces and distributes final minutes within an agreed time scale					
Passes the minute-taking responsibility to another person at the meeting if wanting to make a personal contribution					
Attitude					
Accurate					
Thorough and organized					
Time-conscious					
Confident and professional					
Diplomatic					
Assertive					

Reproduced from *Marvellous Meetings*, Christine Newton, Gower, Aldershot

How well am I doing at meetings?

Questionnaire 3

Use the following check list to gauge your skill at meetings.

For real insight, give a copy of this checklist to the people who attend the meetings you do and ask them for honest feedback.

Scale: **1 = needs work! 5 = excellent every time!** Use n/a wherever a section is not applicable to your role, in self-assessments, and where you are unable to give feedback.

Knowledge	5	4	3	2	1
Meetings procedures and etiquette					
Different behaviour styles (and how to interact with them)					
Presentation and public speaking techniques					
General communication techniques					
Behaviours (skills)					
Punctuality					
Preparation					
Reads all appropriate papers before the meeting					
Prepares thoughts (or makes notes on topics for discussion)					
Prepares notes on personal presentations or topics					
Informs the Chair if unable to attend					
Informs the Chair of time constraints – i.e. if s/he cannot attend the whole meeting					
Keeps to the agenda item					
Keeps focused on the topic under discussion					
Listens without interrupting					
Speaks confidently on own topics					
Makes contributions to other people's topics					
Asks questions in a non-aggressive way					
Respects different opinions					
Disagrees constructively					
Engages in debate					
Helps in the decision-making process					
Attitude					
Confident and professional					
Assertive					
Diplomatic					
Open-minded but decisive when appropriate					
Constructive, even when disagreeing					

Reproduced from *Marvellous Meetings*,
Christine Newton, Gower, Aldershot

Jargon buster – How much do you know?

Questionnaire 4

Don't get confused if someone uses meetings jargon. Check out how much you know! Match the terms listed below with the descriptions given.

Casting vote; Abstention; Lie on the table; *nem dis;* **Address the Chair; Verbatim report; Memorandum and Articles of Association; Executive committee; Quorum; Proxy vote; Board meeting;** *sine die;* **Proposer; Teller; Addendum; Motion; Ad hoc committee;** *in camera;* **Ballot; Standing orders; Unanimous vote; Rider; Terms of reference; Out of order; Annual General Meeting; Ex officio member; Point of order; Tabled; Seconder; Move the closure;** *intra vires;* **Co-opted member; Adjournment;** *ultra vires;* **Extraordinary General Meeting; Standing committee; Postponement; Resolution;** *nem con*

Term	Meaning
	Someone who does not vote for or against a motion.
	A committee formed to deal with a single unit of work. Once this work had been completed, the committee disbands.
	An addition or an alteration to a proposed motion.
	In some formal meetings, those who wish to speak must first address the chairman with 'Mr Chairman' or 'Madam Chairman'.
	The proceedings are suspended and the meeting is reconvened at a later date to complete the unfinished business.
	A statutory meeting held once a year, open to an organization's whole membership.
	A written, secret vote.
	A management meeting of a company's board of directors.
	A second and deciding vote allowed to the chairman when the votes for and against a motion are equal.
	One invited to serve on a committee by the majority of existing members.

Reproduced from *Marvellous Meetings*,
Christine Newton, Gower, Aldershot

Jargon buster – How much do you know? *Questionnaire 4 continued*

Term	Meaning
	One who attends a meeting 'by virtue of their office' but without voting rights, ie secretary to the committee.
	A committee that undertakes the management of an organization.
	A special meeting called to deal with an urgent problem or emergency situation.
	In private – not open to the public.
	Within the legal power or authority of the organization.
	A motion is said to 'lie on the table' when it is decided to take no action upon it.
	Documents in which the structure and management of an organization are set out.
	A formal proposal moved by a member that certain action be taken.
	This phrase is used to indicate the discussion should end and a vote taken.
	No one contradicting, though some may have abstained from voting.
	No one dissenting.
	If a member is not keeping to the point under discussion or is speaking improperly he or she is said to be 'out of order'.
	A member can raise a 'point of order' during a meeting which is a query about a possible infringement of procedure.
	A meeting is held at a later date.
	One who puts forward a motion for discussion at a meeting.
	A vote taken on behalf of someone unable to attend a meeting.

Reproduced from *Marvellous Meetings*,
Christine Newton, Gower, Aldershot

Jargon buster – How much do you know?

Questionnaire 4
concluded

Term	Meaning
	The minimum number of people who must attend to constitute a meeting. This number will be indicated in the Standing Orders.
	A motion passed by a majority vote becomes a resolution. An addition to a resolution (already passed) which must also be voted for.
	One who supports the proposer of a motion before the vote is taken.
	For an indefinite period.
	A permanent committee carrying on day-to-day work.
	The rules of an organization that regulate committee procedure.
	This describes a document that has not been circulated before a meeting but is presented at the meeting.
	One appointed to count votes.
	A statement of the work to be carried out by the members of a committee.
	Outside the legal power or authority of an organization.
	All votes are for or against a motion.
	An exact or word-for-word report.

Reproduced from *Marvellous Meetings*,
Christine Newton, Gower, Aldershot

Work Sheets

1 Running the meeting: communication skills for the Chair

2 Managing behaviour: communication skills for the Chair

3 Constructive communication skills for meetings attendees

Work Sheet 1
Running the meeting: communication skills for the Chair

The following list is a collection of communication skills that a Chair might use when running a successful meeting. Not all the skills listed will be used during every meeting, of course, because the level of formality/informality will determine how the meeting is managed and this, in turn, will determine the type of communication skills required.

Listed in bold print are the stages of a well-run meeting, followed by one or two examples of what might actually be said. *These are not right answers*! They are provided as an example in order to help you generate your own ideas. They act as a catalyst for discussion and practice.

The blank space on the right-hand side of the page has been left for your own notes and alternative or additional phrases.

Stages in running the meeting	What would you say – and how would you say it?
1 **Starting the proceedings.** 'Good afternoon everyone and welcome to ...' 'We have a lot of business to get through today so I shall begin without further delay.'	
2 **Welcoming visitors or new members to the team.** 'Before we begin with this afternoon's business I'd like to introduce ...' 'I have great pleasure in welcoming ...'	
3 **Asking for or stating apologies for absence.** 'Are there any apologies for absence?' 'I've received apologies from ...'	

Reproduced from *Marvellous Meetings*,
Christine Newton, Gower, Aldershot

Running the meeting: communication skills for the Chair

Stages in running the meeting	What would you say – and how would you say it?
4 Stating or clarifying the purpose of the meeting.	'The purpose of this meeting is to …' 'As you can see from our agenda, our objectives today are to …'
5 Checking the minutes have been read and whether there are matters arising.	'Have you all read the minutes of the last meeting?' 'Are there any matters arising from the minutes of the last meeting?'
6 Reducing the disturbance of a late arrival.	(Welcome the late arrival, put him or her in the picture, then go straight back to business.) 'Good afternoon Jo. We've started the meeting and we're on item x. Now as we were saying …' 'Just a minute Sam,' [referring to the current speaker], let's give Jo a moment to sit down then we can give you our full attention.'

Reproduced from *Marvellous Meetings*,
Christine Newton, Gower, Aldershot

Running the meeting: communication skills for the Chair

Stages in running the meeting	What would you say – and how would you say it?
7 Asking for a report of actions taken since the last meeting.	'The first item on the agenda is *xxx*. Jo, you had to *yyy*, how did you get on?' 'Sam, we'd like to hear your report on *zzz*.'
8 Taking a vote.	'Can I have a show of hands for … against … Thank you.' 'How many of you are in favour of that suggestion?'
9 Clarifying the recording of a minute with the minute-taker.	'Did you get all the details for that point, Alex?' 'Alex, I'd like that minute recorded as …'
10 Giving acknowledgement for work done behind the scenes.	'I'd like to congratulate the *xxx* team for *yyy*.' 'I'd like us to show our appreciation for …'
11 Giving thanks for a contribution at the meeting.	'Thank you Sam. That was an excellent presentation/interesting feedback.' 'Thanks, Alex, that was well explained.'

Reproduced from *Marvellous Meetings*, Christine Newton, Gower, Aldershot

Running the meeting: communication skills for the Chair

Stages in running the meeting	What would you say – and how would you say it?
12 Challenging the introduction of 'any other business'.	'Alex, if you want us to spend time on that topic, I'd like you to make sure it's on the agenda for next week.'
	'Sam, that item's really outside the purpose of this meeting.'
13 Checking that all actions to be taken before the next meeting are understood and agreed.	'Is everyone clear about what's expected of them before the next meeting?'
	'Does anyone have any questions about the actions they've been assigned?'
14 Checking that all essential business has been dealt with.	'Let me quickly go through the action points against each agenda item.'
	'Have I covered everything?'
15 Closing the meeting and agreeing the date of the next.	'Thank you everyone and our next meeting will be on …'
	'Thank you all. Now let's check our diaries for our next meeting.'

Reproduced from *Marvellous Meetings*, Christine Newton, Gower, Aldershot

Work Sheet 2

Managing behaviour: communication skills for the Chair

The following list is a collection of communication skills that a Chair might use when running a successful meeting. The skills in this list are all connected with managing the behaviour of the meetings attendees.

The behaviour management tactic is printed in bold, followed by one or two examples of what might actually be said. *These are not right answers!* They are provided as an example of a **constructive** and **assertive** communication style in order to help you generate your own ideas. They act as a catalyst for discussion and practice. Notice how often the other person's name is used within the examples.

The blank space on the right-hand side of the page has been left for your own notes and alternative or additional phrases.

Managing behaviour in meetings	What would you say – and how would you say it?
1 Clarifying a point that's just been discussed. 'So, am I right in thinking that what you mean is …' 'So as I understand it, you are suggesting that we should …'	
2 Asking for clarification from a speaker. 'Jo, will you clarify that last point for us please.' 'Sam, I'm not sure I fully understand the implications of your last statement. Will you clarify your position please.'	
3 Summarizing. 'Let's stop for a moment and summarize the position so far.' 'Before we go on with the next item of business I want to summarize the decisions made up to this point.'	

Reproduced from *Marvellous Meetings*,
Christine Newton, Gower, Aldershot

Managing behaviour: communication skills for the Chair

Managing behaviour in meetings	What would you say – and how would you say it?
4 Refocusing a waffling speaker.	
'Sam, we don't have time to go into that much detail. Could you give us a *brief* outline of your plan.'	
'Jo, we're running out of time on this item. We need to move on.'	
5 Keeping everyone to the agenda item.	
'Jo, that's very interesting but we need to get back to the agenda item.'	
'Please stick to the point everyone. We have 15 minutes to concentrate on the decision we have to make.'	
6 Dealing with a discussion that's outside the scope of the agreed agenda, and is not relevant to the business of the meeting.	
'Jo, you've raised something we need to discuss outside this meeting. Let's get together at the end of the evening.'	
'Sam, this is obviously important to you but it's not part of the business in hand. We'll talk about it later.'	

Reproduced from *Marvellous Meetings*,
Christine Newton, Gower, Aldershot

Work Sheet 2 continued

Managing behaviour: communication skills for the Chair

Managing behaviour in meetings	What would you say – and how would you say it?
7 **Challenging someone who's using subjective statements, exaggerating and making assumptions.** 'What do you mean *precisely*?' 'Where did you get the evidence/ figures/ background on that, Jo?' 'Is that fact, your opinion or an assumption, Sam?'	
8 **Dealing with a small clique of people who are talking independently of the meeting.** 'Excuse me Jo, Sam and Alex. Are you discussing something that we should all hear?' 'Excuse me. Would you come back to the main discussion. We need your opinions on this matter.'	
9 **Dealing with someone who is nervous and quiet.** 'Now, Sam, I know you have some experience in this area. What do you think about it?' 'Alex, you were telling me earlier about *xxx*. Tell me again what you were saying.' *(Make a particular point of thanking a nervous speaker for talking.)*	

Reproduced from *Marvellous Meetings*,
Christine Newton, Gower, Aldershot

Work Sheet 2 continued

Managing behaviour: communication skills for the Chair

Managing behaviour in meetings	What would you say – and how would you say it?
10 Dealing with someone who's not participating (disruptive body language; dismissive of the proceedings).	'Jo, you're drumming your fingers on the table. You're giving me the impression that you're not at all interested in this meeting. Is that right?' 'Sam, I appreciate this might not be your own subject area, but we'd really appreciate your help and co-operation right now.'
11 Giving credit back where it belongs after someone has pinched someone else's idea.	'You're absolutely right Sam. But wasn't that the point Jo was making a moment ago? Jo …?' 'Jo, is that what you were saying just now?'
12 Dealing with someone who's upset.	'Sam, I can see you're upset about this. Nevertheless we do need to get to the point.' 'Jo, I can see you're upset by this. Would you like to take a moment to compose yourself, then we'll return to the discussion.'

Reproduced from *Marvellous Meetings*,
Christine Newton, Gower, Aldershot

Work Sheet 2 concluded

Managing behaviour: communication skills for the Chair

Managing behaviour in meetings	What would you say – and how would you say it?
13 Dealing with someone who's angry.	
'Jo, I can see this is important to you, but we can't talk about the solutions when all we do is go over the problem.'	
'You have every right to be angry. I understand how you feel. I felt the same way at first, but later, when I thought about it, I found …'	
14 Dealing with aggressive, rude or offensive behaviour.	
'Jo, I'm aware this means a lot to you, nevertheless please don't let your enthusiasm get in the way of your professional courtesy.'	
'Alex, that sounded aggressive/ rude/offensive/ offhand. Is that what you intended?'	
15 Encouraging effective meetings behaviour in future.	
'Thanks everyone for being prompt, being prepared and sticking to the point. We've finished our meeting on time.'	
'That was a good meeting! Well organized, well presented and on time! Many thanks.'	

Reproduced from *Marvellous Meetings*,
Christine Newton, Gower, Aldershot

Work Sheet 3

Constructive communication skills for meetings attendees

The following list is a collection of communication skills that confident and competent meetings attendees are likely to use in a range of circumstances. The suggested phrases given below do not represent *right answers*! They are designed to provide examples of the type of approach that can work when used appropriately, that is **constructive** and **assertive**, and help stimulate your imagination and creativity.

The blank space on the right-hand side of the page has been left for your own notes and alternative or additional phrases.

Constructive communication at meetings	What would you say – and how would you say it?
1 **Stating an opinion confidently, using a convincing, persuasive and authoritative tone of voice.** 'I think ...' 'I feel ...' 'I believe ...' 'I would like ...'	
2 **Making a proposal or a suggestion.** 'I propose ...' 'I suggest ...' 'Let's consider ...' 'How about ...'	
3 **Making positive opening comments in preparation for giving a report.** 'It's been a busy month and I'm delighted to be able to tell you ...' 'As you all know, last month we planned ... Now I can report on the outcome of those plans.'	

Reproduced from *Marvellous Meetings*,
Christine Newton, Gower, Aldershot

Work Sheet 3 continued

Constructive communication skills for meetings attendees

Constructive communication at meetings	What would you say – and how would you say it?
4 Making positive opening comments in preparation for giving a presentation. 'It gives me great pleasure …' 'I'm really delighted to be able to …' 'Good afternoon everyone. My name is Jo, and during the next 10 minutes I plan to …'	
5 Seeking information on someone else's topic. 'I'd like to know more about …' 'I'm not familiar with that subject. What's the background to it?'	
6 Asking someone to clarify something you don't understand. 'Jo, what do you mean by that? How does that work?' 'Sam, I don't understand. Will you go through that again please?'	
7 Interrupting someone who has just interrupted you – regaining the 'floor'. 'That may be true, but as I was saying …' 'Jo, just a minute. I want to finish my point. Now as I was saying …' 'Sam, I appreciate that's important to you, and we can come back to that, but I want to continue with my point.'	

Reproduced from *Marvellous Meetings*, Christine Newton, Gower, Aldershot

Work Sheet 3 continued

Constructive communication skills for meetings attendees

Constructive communication at meetings	What would you say – and how would you say it?

8 Interrupting someone who is waffling off the subject.

'Excuse me Jo, but I think we've moved away from the subject under discussion.'

'Just a minute, Sam. I want to finish my point. Now as I was saying …'

9 Dealing with being ignored.

'Excuse me. I'd like to make a comment here.'

'Just a moment. I'd like to ask about …'

'Excuse me. Before you move on, I really would like to know what you think about …'

10 Building on a colleague's idea in order to change their opinion and do it your way!

'That's a good idea – but I wonder, have you also considered linking in …'

'That would be a good start – then we could move in the direction of …'

'That's great in principle. Now let's consider the detail.'

Reproduced from *Marvellous Meetings*, Christine Newton, Gower, Aldershot

Constructive communication skills for meetings attendees

Constructive communication at meetings	What would you say – and how would you say it?
11 Encouraging a colleague by helping them build on their original idea. 'That's a good idea. What do you plan to do after that?' 'How will you develop that idea?' 'How are you going to make sure everyone's committed to that?'	
12 Dealing with someone's aggressive behaviour. 'Alex! That sounded aggressive. What exactly did you mean?' 'I don't think that's a very constructive point of view, Jo.' 'Mr Chairman! I think we're getting too personal about this. Let's stop for a moment.'	
13 Standing your ground in the face of a personal put-down. THEM: 'Do you expect me to take that seriously?' YOU: 'Yes. I'm putting this forward as a serious proposal.' THEM: 'That's stupid.' YOU: 'I don't agree with you. I think it's a good idea and worthy of some consideration.'	

Reproduced from *Marvellous Meetings*, Christine Newton, Gower, Aldershot

Work Sheet 3 continued

Constructive communication skills for meetings attendees

Constructive communication at meetings	What would you say – and how would you say it?

14 **Standing your ground in the face of a disagreement.**

'That may be so, but I still believe …'

'I appreciate you have a different opinion, but my experience tells me …'

'I can understand why you might think that way, but from my perspective …'

15 **Expressing your unwillingness to accept an idea or to go along with something you don't agree with.**

'I don't feel comfortable with that.'

'No. That's not something I'm prepared to go along with. What I *am* prepared to do is …'

16 **Disagreeing with someone's point of view.**

'Jo, I appreciate your point of view but I don't agree with you.'

'Sam, I see the situation quite differently.'

'Alex, that's not how I see the situation. I don't share that opinion.'

Reproduced from *Marvellous Meetings*, Christine Newton, Gower, Aldershot

Work Sheet 3 continued

Constructive communication skills for meetings attendees

Constructive communication at meetings	What would you say – and how would you say it?

17 Using 'reflective listening' (repeating the words or ideas of the other person).

THEM: 'I'm not very happy about that idea and I think it's too expensive.'

YOU: 'Well, I'm sorry to hear that you're not very happy about this and although I can understand why you think it's too expensive, I still believe …'

18 Dealing with someone who has just pinched your idea and presented it as their own.

'That's a great idea and exactly what I was saying a moment ago. Now as I was saying …'

'I agree with that entirely. Did you get that from the report I sent you last week?'

'Jo, I hope you're going to credit me as the originator of that idea!'

19 Dealing with an unskilled Chair – sticking to the agenda item.

'Madam Chairman, I think we've gone off at a tangent. I'd like to get back to …'

'Jo, we've gone off track. Can we get back to …'

Reproduced from *Marvellous Meetings*, Christine Newton, Gower, Aldershot

Work Sheet 3 concluded

Constructive communication skills for meetings attendees

Constructive communication at meetings	What would you say – and how would you say it?
20 Dealing with an unskilled Chair – moving the business on.	
'Excuse me, Chair. I'm concerned about time. At this rate we won't get all our business finished. Can we move on?'	
'Sam, it's getting late. Can we come to a decision on this?'	
'Alex, I feel we're losing the thread and running out of time. Can we summarize and move on?'	

Reproduced from *Marvellous Meetings*,
Christine Newton, Gower, Aldershot

Cards

Skill-building Cards for the Chair: Running the meeting

Skill-building Cards for the Chair: Managing behaviour

Skill-building Cards for Meetings Attendees: Constructive and assertive communication skills

Skill-building Cards: Bad behaviour at meetings

Discussion-generating Cards: What would you do or say?

Running the Meeting Communication Skills for the Chair – 1 Welcome attendees to the meeting and start the proceedings.	**Running the Meeting Communication Skills for the Chair – 2** Welcome a visitor to your meeting or introduce new members to your project team meeting.
Running the Meeting Communication Skills for the Chair – 3 Ask for apologies for absence.	**Running the Meeting Communication Skills for the Chair – 4** State or clarify the point and purpose of the meeting.
Running the Meeting Communication Skills for the Chair – 5 Check that the minutes from the last meeting have been read, and ask if there are 'any matters arising'.	**Running the Meeting Communication Skills for the Chair – 6** Reduce the disturbance of a late arrival. (Sam had been stuck in traffic because of an accident and had telephoned ahead.)
Running the Meeting Communication Skills for the Chair – 7 Ask for a report of actions taken since the last meeting.	**Running the Meeting Communication Skills for the Chair – 8** Take a vote.

Reproduced from *Marvellous Meetings*,
Christine Newton, Gower, Aldershot

Running the Meeting Communication Skills for the Chair – 9

Clarify the recording of a minute with the minute taker.

Running the Meeting Communication Skills for the Chair – 10

Give acknowledgement for work done behind the scenes.

Running the Meeting Communication Skills for the Chair – 11

Give thanks for a contribution at the meeting.

Running the Meeting Communication Skills for the Chair – 12

Challenge the introduction of 'any other business'.

Running the Meeting Communication Skills for the Chair – 13

Check that all actions to be taken before the next meeting are understood and agreed.

Running the Meeting Communication Skills for the Chair – 14

Check that all essential business has been dealt with.

Running the Meeting Communication Skills for the Chair – 15

Close the meeting and agree the date of the next.

Reproduced from *Marvellous Meetings*, Christine Newton, Gower, Aldershot

Managing Behaviour Communication Skills for the Chair – 1 Clarify a point that's just been discussed.	**Managing Behaviour Communication Skills for the Chair – 2** Ask for clarification from the previous speaker.
Managing Behaviour Communication Skills for the Chair – 3 Summarize the proceedings so far.	**Managing Behaviour Communication Skills for the Chair – 4** Refocus a waffling speaker.
Managing Behaviour Communication Skills for the Chair – 5 Keep everyone to the agenda item.	**Managing Behaviour Communication Skills for the Chair – 6** Deal with a discussion that's outside the scope of the agenda, and is not relevant to the business of the meeting.
Managing Behaviour Communication Skills for the Chair – 7 Challenge someone who's using subjective statements, exaggerating and making assumptions.	**Managing Behaviour Communication Skills for the Chair – 8** Deal with a small clique of people who are talking independently of the meeting.

Reproduced from *Marvellous Meetings*, Christine Newton, Gower, Aldershot

Managing Behaviour Communication Skills for the Chair – 9

Deal with someone who is nervous and quiet.

Managing Behaviour Communication Skills for the Chair – 10

Deal with someone who's not participating (disruptive body language; dismissive of the proceedings …).

Managing Behaviour Communication Skills for the Chair – 11

Give credit back where it belongs after someone has pinched someone else's idea.

Managing Behaviour Communication Skills for the Chair – 12

Deal with someone who's upset.

Managing Behaviour Communication Skills for the Chair – 13

Deal with someone who's angry.

Managing Behaviour Communication Skills for the Chair – 14

Deal with aggressive, rude or offensive behaviour.

Managing Behaviour Communication Skills for the Chair – 15

Encourage effective meetings behaviour in future.

Reproduced from *Marvellous Meetings*, Christine Newton, Gower, Aldershot

Constructive and Assertive Communication Skills – 1

State your opinion confidently, using a convincing, persuasive and authoritative tone of voice. Use 'I' statements.

Constructive and Assertive Communication Skills – 2

Make a proposal or a suggestion.

Constructive and Assertive Communication Skills – 3

You are about to give a report. Make sure your opening statements are positive.

Constructive and Assertive Communication Skills – 4

You are about to give a presentation. Make sure your opening comments are positive.

Constructive and Assertive Communication Skills – 5

Ask for information on someone else's topic.

Constructive and Assertive Communication Skills – 6

Ask someone to clarify something you don't understand.

Constructive and Assertive Communication Skills – 7

Interrupt someone who's just interrupted you. In other words, regain the 'floor'.

Constructive and Assertive Communication Skills – 8

Interrupt someone who's waffling off the subject.

Reproduced from *Marvellous Meetings*, Christine Newton, Gower, Aldershot

Constructive and Assertive Communication Skills – 9 Deal with being ignored.	**Constructive and Assertive Communication Skills – 10** Build on a colleague's idea in order to change their opinion and do it your way.
Constructive and Assertive Communication Skills – 11 Encourage a colleague by helping them build on their original idea.	**Constructive and Assertive Communication Skills – 12** Deal with someone's aggressive behaviour.
Constructive and Assertive Communication Skills – 13 Stand your ground in the face of a personal put-down.	**Constructive and Assertive Communication Skills – 14** Stand your ground in the face of a disagreement.
Constructive and Assertive Communication Skills – 15 Express your unwillingness to accept an idea or to go along with something you don't agree with.	**Constructive and Assertive Communication Skills – 16** Disagree with someone else's point of view.

Reproduced from *Marvellous Meetings*,
Christine Newton, Gower, Aldershot

Constructive and Assertive Communication Skills – 17

Use reflective listening – repeat the words or ideas of the other person.

Constructive and Assertive Communication Skills – 18

Deal with someone who's just pinched your idea and presented it as their own.

Constructive and Assertive Communication Skills – 19

Deal with an unskilled Chair – get him or her to stick to the point.

Constructive and Assertive Communication Skills – 20

Deal with an unskilled Chair – get him or her to move the business on.

Bad Behaviour at Meetings – 1

Arrive late for the meeting and be disruptive as you sit at the table.

Bad Behaviour at Meetings – 2

Introduce a topic of 'any other business' completely unconnected to the main business of the meeting. Make one or two attempts to keep your topic until you back down.

Bad Behaviour at Meetings – 3

Join in the current discussion but use the most complicated language that you can! Try to dazzle the crowd with your broad vocabulary!

Bad Behaviour at Meetings – 4

Join in the current discussion but from a position of not really knowing the subject matter. Disguise your 'not knowing' by going round in circles, off at a tangent, bringing up complications …

Bad Behaviour at Meetings – 5

Listen to the current topic then go off at a tangent.

Bad Behaviour at Meetings – 6

Go off the agenda once or twice. Perhaps go into day-dream mode, or start a non-connected thought with *'That reminds me of the time ..'*

Bad Behaviour at Meetings – 7

Make comments that are subjective, exaggerated and full of assumptions in a negative way, using words like: *always (going wrong), never (works), totally (useless), completely (inadequate).*

Bad Behaviour at Meetings – 8

Play the cynical disbeliever. Use language such as: *'We tried it before, it didn't work then.' 'That won't work.' 'Can't see the point.'* (Choose a time when you'll be able to argue your case.)

Reproduced from *Marvellous Meetings*, Christine Newton, Gower, Aldershot

Bad Behaviour at Meetings – 9

Make comments that are subjective, exaggerated and full of assumptions – in a positive way – using words like: *'Absolutely fantastic' 'Don't think about it – just do it!' 'That's bound to work.'*

Bad Behaviour at Meetings – 10

Use disruptive body language: drum your fingers on the table, click a ball-point pen, turn your chair sideways to the table …

Bad Behaviour at Meetings – 11

As soon as the meeting starts, fold your arms, look around the room, look out of the window, look at your watch – anything *except* participate.

Bad Behaviour at Meetings – 12

Engage in a private conversation with one or two people sitting next to you. Whisper and laugh in a disruptive way.

Bad Behaviour at Meetings – 13

Participate at the beginning of the meeting but as things progress, start to give out body language signals that you're not interested. Do this subtly.

Bad Behaviour at Meetings – 14

Wait until one of your colleagues is in the middle of a topic – then interrupt by just talking over them. Repeat as many times as you can – until you feel they or the Chair have 'controlled' this behaviour.

Bad Behaviour at Meetings – 15

Listen out for a good idea or a comment that's not been picked up on by the meeting. A few minutes later represent that idea as your own.

Bad Behaviour at Meetings – 16

Listen out for something that you can 'get upset' about. (*Behaviour suggestion: fold arms, sniff, shake head sideways …*)

Reproduced from *Marvellous Meetings*, Christine Newton, Gower, Aldershot

Bad Behaviour at Meetings – 17

Give out body language signals to suggest that you feel nervous.
(Behaviour suggestion: little eye contact, fidget with fingers, pencils etc., don't speak voluntarily …)

Bad Behaviour at Meetings – 18

Behave in a rude, offensive or offhand manner to one of your colleagues.

Bad Behaviour at Meetings – 19

Become angry about the way a certain topic is progressing. Behave aggressively towards one of the meetings attendees.

Bad Behaviour at Meetings – 20

Find an opportunity to say, *'Don't be ridiculous!'*

Bad Behaviour at Meetings – 21

Say *'I don't understand'* at the first opportunity. Keep stating that you don't understand (suggestions: *'No, I'm not really sure'*, *'I can't see what you're getting at'* …) until the third set of explanations!

Bad Behaviour at Meetings – 22

Respond to one of your colleague's comments with *'Come on, give us a break!'*

Bad Behaviour at Meetings – 23

Ignore someone by pretending you haven't heard them.

Bad Behaviour at Meetings – 24

Find an opportunity to say:
'Don't you ever engage your brain before you open your mouth?'

When challenged (as you should be) respond: *'I was only joking. Can't you take a joke?'*

Reproduced from *Marvellous Meetings*,
Christine Newton, Gower, Aldershot

What would you do or say? – 1

You notice that three new people are attending your meeting but the chairman has not welcomed them, introduced them or even mentioned them.

What would you do or say? – 2

You are often asked to attend and participate in meetings that do not have a prepared agenda. Often there is no stated objective for the meeting.

What would you do or say? – 3

You are often asked to attend meetings at which it is usual for people *not* to have prepared in advance – i.e. they have not read the minutes or any accompanying papers.

(Optional complication: the Chair is equally at fault here.)

What would you do or say? – 4

It is usual practice to allow interruptions in your meetings: messages are delivered; the business telephones ring; mobile phones ring.

What would you do or say? – 5

You have a Chair who often wanders off the published agenda into a 'world of her own'.

What would you do or say? – 6

When the actions from the last meeting are reported upon, one of your colleagues – yet again – has not fulfilled his/her commitment. The team leader lets this go – yet again.

What would you do or say? – 7

Punctuality is a constant problem for your meetings. You never start on time.

What would you do or say? – 8

Booking meetings can be a 'nightmare'. Getting several busy people together is always difficult. What ways can you suggest to ease this problem?

Reproduced from *Marvellous Meetings*,
Christine Newton, Gower, Aldershot

What would you do or say? – 9

Your meeting agendas are always too long. You can never complete the business and often topics are given only a superficial hearing.

What would you do or say? – 10

Your meetings are always over-running. This disrupts the rest of your schedule and often makes you late for subsequent meetings.

What would you do or say? – 11

You feel that the minutes of your meetings are often inaccurate and sometimes show the bias of the minute-taker.

What would you do or say? – 12

You have a member of your team who uses the forum of your team meetings to voice personal grievances – to the exclusion of moving the team business forward.

What would you do or say? – 13

You feel that the minutes taken at your team meetings are too lengthy and detailed. You feel that a brief summary and a simple action list would be more appropriate. You feel that the time taken to write detailed minutes and the time taken to read them could be better used.

What would you do or say? – 14

Your team leader is not particularly good at leading your team meetings.

What would you do or say? – 15

You want to make an important point at your next meeting but experience tells you that the more dominant among your colleagues will not let you 'get a word in edgewise'.

What would you do or say? – 16

You are asked to attend a very long meeting, most of which is irrelevant to you but you have to stay because your contribution is usually timetabled three-quarters of the way through.

Reproduced from *Marvellous Meetings*,
Christine Newton, Gower, Aldershot

What would you do or say? – 17

You are nervous about speaking up at meetings. You feel that people often do not give your ideas enough credit or take you seriously. You want to change this situation.

What would you do or say? – 18

Although your meetings are well managed, 'any other business' seems to have become a key feature lately. This is making your meetings less effective because members of the team have not prepared their thoughts on these new matters.

What would you do or say? – 19

Although you are not the Chair or the team leader at your meetings, you think that your meetings would be more effective if everyone 'bought into' a **Code of Conduct** for meetings. How might you suggest this and follow it through?

What would you do or say? – 20

Someone's just suggested to you that saying *'I don't understand'* at a meeting or asking for clarification on a topic is a sign of weakness and bad for your career prospects. How might you respond?

What would you do or say? – 21

What's the best (assertive) way of refocusing a waffling speaker and keeping him or her to the agenda item?

What would you do or say? – 22

What's the best (assertive) way of responding to someone who wants to introduce a topic that's not on the agenda?

What would you do or say? – 23

What's the best (assertive) way of challenging someone who has a habit of making subjective statements, exaggerating and making assumptions?

What would you do or say? – 24

What's the best (assertive) way of dealing with a small group of people who whisper and chat together during the course of a meeting?

Reproduced from *Marvellous Meetings*,
Christine Newton, Gower, Aldershot

What would you do or say? – 25

What's the best (assertive) way of helping and supporting someone who's nervous and quiet at meetings?

What would you do or say? – 26

What's the best (assertive) way of dealing with someone who is disruptive at meetings (that is, who uses distracting body language, drums their fingers, clicks pens, sighs …)?

What would you do or say? – 27

What's the best (assertive) way of responding when someone has pinched your own idea and presented it as their own – especially if the meeting gives them the credit for it?

What would you do or say? – 28

What's the best (assertive) way of responding when you notice that someone has pinched someone else's idea – especially if the meeting gives them the credit for it?

What would you do or say? – 29

What's the best (assertive) way of dealing with someone who's upset?

What would you do or say? – 30

What's the best (assertive) way of dealing with someone who's angry?

What would you do or say? – 31

What's the best (assertive) way of dealing with someone who's rude or offensive?

What would you do or say? – 32

What's the best (assertive) way of encouraging good meetings behaviour in the future?

Reproduced from *Marvellous Meetings*,
Christine Newton, Gower, Aldershot

What would you do or say? – 33

What's the best (assertive) way of presenting yourself at meetings, especially when you want to sound confident, convincing, persuasive and authoritative?

What would you do or say? – 34

What's the best (assertive) way of making a proposal or a suggestion at a meeting so that you sound confident and professional?

What would you do or say? – 35

What's the best (assertive) way of making your opening remarks when you are about to give a report or make a presentation at a meeting?

What would you do or say? – 36

What's the best (assertive) way of expressing the fact that you don't understand or of asking for clarification of a topic?

What would you do or say? – 37

What's the best (assertive) way of interrupting someone who's just interrupted you, so that you can regain the floor and continue with your point?

What would you do or say? – 38

What's the best (assertive) way of interrupting someone who keeps wandering off the subject?

What would you do or say? – 39

What's the best (assertive) way of dealing with being ignored?

What would you do or say? – 40

What's the best (assertive) way of building on a colleague's idea in order to change their opinion and get them to do it your way?

Reproduced from *Marvellous Meetings*,
Christine Newton, Gower, Aldershot

What would you do or say? – 41

What's the best (assertive) way of encouraging a colleague by helping them build on their own idea?

What would you do or say? – 42

What's the best (assertive) way of dealing with someone's aggressive behaviour?

What would you do or say? – 43

What's the best (assertive) way of standing your ground in the face of a personal 'put-down'?

What would you do or say? – 44

What's the best (assertive) way of standing your ground in the face of a disagreement?

What would you do or say? – 45

What's the best (assertive) way of expressing your unwillingness to accept an idea or to go along with something you don't agree with?

What would you do or say? – 46

What's the best (assertive) way of disagreeing with someone's point of view?

What would you do or say? – 47

How can 'reflective listening' be used to help someone stand their ground in a discussion?

What would you do or say? – 48

What's the best (assertive) way of dealing with an unskilled Chair who is not taking control of the organization of a meeting?

Reproduced from *Marvellous Meetings*,
Christine Newton, Gower, Aldershot

What would you do or say? – 49 What's the best (assertive) way of dealing with an unskilled Chair who has no time management skills?	**What would you do or say? – 50** What's the best (assertive) way of dealing with an unskilled Chair who doesn't challenge non-constructive behaviour at a meeting?

Appendix 1: Meeting intervention strategies

The question of how to transfer the learning of skills or ideas from a training session to the work place is one that is often faced by the trainer, the facilitator and, indeed, the training participants themselves. This resource seeks to explore this issue.

The examples we've provided are simply enlarged samples of readily available clip-art from one of the most common word processing systems. These can be printed on card and fixed to sticks or stands to act as 'flags' during a meeting:

- The mouth – when someone is chattering too much or going off the topic.
- The wristwatch – when someone is taking too much time.

The fun of this exercise is to encourage your training participants to come up with intervention strategies that they can successfully use in their own meetings.

Remember the beach ball? This is an idea that's been in circulation for several years. The only person who can speak at a meeting is the one holding the beach ball. Well, that's an intervention strategy!

Appendix 1: Meeting intervention strategies

Meeting Intervention Strategy

Reproduced from *Marvellous Meetings*,
Christine Newton, Gower, Aldershot

Meeting Intervention Strategy

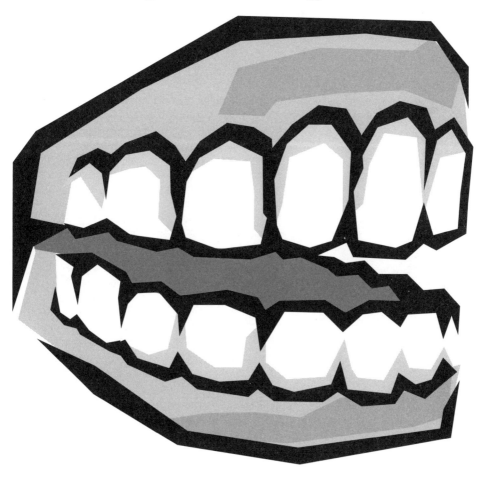

Reproduced from *Marvellous Meetings*,
Christine Newton, Gower, Aldershot

Meeting Intervention Strategy

Reproduced from *Marvellous Meetings*,
Christine Newton, Gower, Aldershot

Appendix 2: Assertive techniques

Assertive techniques contained within Work Sheet 3 and Skill-building Cards for Meeting Attendees

The communication style used throughout this Appendix is based on assertiveness, that is standing one's ground confidently and authoritatively while never violating the rights of the other person. The suggested language used is not presented as a 'right answer' but is given as an example of how an assertive technique might be used and expressed.

The list below is also aiming to give you, the trainer or facilitator, further ideas on how these assertive techniques might be applied.

1. Owning your own opinion. Use 'I' statements to state opinions non-aggressively but firmly. Portraying a confident image. Dealing with conflict. Negotiating.
2. Using a confident tone of voice. Using non-apologetic language. Speaking up confidently. Portraying a confident image. Negotiating.
3. Positive language. Preparing others to receive messages positively. Portraying a confident image.

4. Positive language. Preparing others to receive messages positively. Portraying a confident image. Negotiating.
5. Asking for information when you need it – confidently. Portraying a confident image. Negotiating.
6. Asking for clarification when you need it – without embarrassment. Portraying a confident image. Negotiating.
7. Standing your ground, verbally. Portraying a confident image. Dealing with conflict. Negotiating.
8. Re-directing someone else, non-aggressively.
9. Not allowing behaviours that you don't like to continue. Using 'break-in' phrases. Dealing with conflict. Negotiating.
10. Using 'building' techniques as an alternative to argument. Negotiating.
11. Using 'building' techniques to direct conversations in your desired direction. Controlling the debate. Negotiating.
12. Not allowing behaviours that you don't like to continue. Dealing with conflict. Negotiating.
13. Not 'buying into' other people's negativity or aggression. Standing your ground. Responding to the words said, not the aggression. Portraying a confident image. Dealing with conflict. Negotiating.
14. Not being intimidated. Maintaining confidence during a disagreement. Using validation as a response. Portraying a confident image. Dealing with conflict. Negotiating.
15. How to say 'No'. Dealing with conflict. Negotiating.
16. How to disagree constructively. Portraying a confident image. Dealing with conflict. Negotiating.
17. The power of reflective listening when needing to take control of a discussion or debate. Portraying a confident image. Negotiating.
18. Standing up for yourself and your worth as an individual. Dealing with conflict.
19. Taking control of a situation.
20. Taking control of a situation. Talking factually and avoiding an emotional outburst.

Appendix 3: Some ideas on using the skill-building cards

1. You, the trainer, select the cards that you need to make your training point or to build skill in a particular area.
2. Ask the trainees to select the cards containing the areas they wish to develop.
3. Shuffle the cards and deal them randomly.
4. Decide how many times the card should be 'played' during each meeting: should it be played only once and then turned over or played again and again?
5. For games and competitions you can allocate points for each card. Once a card has been played the point is gained.

Appendix 4: Some ideas on using the skill-building tasks

Appendix 4: Additional training themes

The following matrix suggests which of the resources you might use to develop sessions on other training issues related to meetings.

	Time Management	Organizational Skills	Presentation Skills	Dealing with Conflict	Negotiating
Information Sheet 1: Principles of effective meetings	YES	YES	YES		
Information Sheet 2: Documentation – the agenda	YES	YES			
Information Sheet 3: Documentation – the minutes	YES	YES			
Information Sheet 4: The action plan	YES	YES			
Check List 1: Responsibilities of the Chair		YES			

	Time Management	Organizational Skills	Presentation Skills	Dealing with Conflict	Negotiating
Check List 2: Responsibilities of the minute-taker		YES			
Check List 3: Responsibilities of the meetings attendees					
Check List 4: Jargon buster					
Questionnaire 1: How well am I doing as Chair?		YES			
Questionnaire 2: How well am I doing as minute-taker?					
Questionnaire 3: How well am I doing at meetings?					
Questionnaire 4: Jargon buster: how much do you know?					
Work Sheet 1: Running the meeting	YES	YES			
Work Sheet 2: Managing behaviour	YES	YES		YES	
Work Sheet 3: Constructive and assertive communication skills for meetings attendees		YES	YES	YES	YES
Skill-building Cards: Running the meeting					

	Time Management	Organizational Skills	Presentation Skills	Dealing with Conflict	Negotiating
Skill-building Cards: Managing behaviour					
Skill-building Cards: Constructive and assertive communication skills					
Bad Behaviour Cards					
Discussion-generating Cards	YES	YES	YES	YES	YES
Appendix 1: Meeting intervention strategies	YES				

58½ Ways to Improvise in Training

Improvisation Games and Activities for Workshops, Courses and Team Meetings

Paul Z Jackson

Each of these games and activities generates what Paul Jackson calls 'Impro Energy', a current that runs between participants. You recognize 'Impro Energy' when you see people who are clearly 'in the moment', alert to whatever is going on in the here and now. At its best, it creates an event in which the quality of work is both high and seemingly effortless. At all levels, it is great fun - a rich mixture of preparation and spontaneity.

The games in this collection can be used in a variety of ways. A physical activity warms up limbs and might also break down barriers between group members. A verbal activity might be an exercise in creativity as well as intellectual dexterity.

More than simply icebreakers, they are designed as a vehicle for content. There are always links between the game and the subject of the workshop at a metaphorical level. The Ping-pong process, for example, can be positioned to show how a relaxed attitude to making mistakes often results in fewer errors.

The questions provided in the debriefing section that accompanies each game provide the means for making these connections. They offer prompts for generating insights, which you can then link to similar or parallel experiences in the workplace.

Whether you are running a training session, workshop or a team meeting, Paul Jackson's varied collection of games and activities will help you to create an environment of improvisation and experiment, of imagination and energy, and of laughter and commitment. What better way to engage anyone in the process of learning!

Gower

75 Ways to Liven Up Your Training

A Collection of Energizing Activities

Martin Orridge

Most of the activities in Martin Orridge's book require little in the way of either expertise or equipment. Yet they provide a powerful way of stimulating creativity, helping people to enjoy learning, or simply injecting new momentum into the training process.

Each activity is presented under a standard set of headings, including a brief description, a statement of purpose, likely duration, a note of any materials required and detailed instructions for running the event. In addition there are suggestions for debriefing and possible variations.

To help users to select the most appropriate activities they are arranged in the book by type or process. There are exercises for individuals, pairs and large groups and they range from icebreakers to closing events.

Trainers, managers, team leaders and anyone responsible for developing people will find this volume a rich store-house of ideas.

Gower

90 Brain Teasers for Trainers

Graham Roberts-Phelps and Anne McDougall

The activities and exercises in this collection are designed to broaden perception, and improve learning, thinking and problem-solving skills. Using them is also a valuable way to boost energy levels at the beginning, middle or end of any training session.

The collection will help any group engage all five senses in their learning, and develop creative and lateral thinking, word usage, mental dexterity and cooperative team skills. Most of the activities require no more than a flip chart or OHP to run. And because they need only a few moments preparation, they can be planned into sessions in advance, or simply introduced to fill gaps, or to signal a change of direction, as appropriate.

Trainers, teachers and team leaders will find *Brain Teasers for Trainers* a rich source of simple, flexible, and easy-to-use exercises, as well as the inspiration for their own variants.

Gower

Bullying in the Workplace

An Organizational Toolkit

Elaine Douglas

Bullying at work is widespread and its effect can result in low morale, high staff turnover, increased sickness absence, low productivity and ultimately expensive legal costs. This practical and pragmatic toolkit is a comprehensive guide to identifying, understanding and eradicating the problem. It will help you to set up and manage an efficient anti-bullying policy ensuring commitment throughout the organization. Alongside this are strategies and techniques for managers and professionals to help their staff address how to work with victims and bullies.

The tools available range from sophisticated questionnaires to helpful methods, which individuals can adapt to deal with a bully themselves. The emphasis is always on providing sensible, problem-solving advice. Whether you are a human resource or a line manager, *Bullying in the Workplace* will show you how to create a climate in which people are not threatened or frightened and are therefore able to work happily and productively as a team.

Gower

Developing Your People

Easy-to-use Activities for Improving Management Skills

Mike Woodcock and Dave Francis

As the trend towards 'learning organizations' accelerates, managers are increasingly expected to be 'people developers'. It is no longer enough to identify training needs and recommend external training courses. More and more training today is ongoing, and often takes place through projects undertaken at work, designed to stretch and challenge existing skills or competencies. So today's manager needs, more than ever before, to know how to bring out the full potential of his or her people on both a day-to-day and a long-term basis.

Mike Woodcock and Dave Francis have recognized this in compiling *Developing Your People*, a collection of 36 training activities designed to help any senior manager identify the 'blockages' to performance of individuals, and address them through interactive exercises. An initial survey helps pinpoint key needs, and an index then leads you to the relevant activities. Each activity includes step-by-step instructions on how to prepare and run the exercise, together with photocopiable masters of any handouts or other material needed by participants.

This collection of ready-to-use material puts tried and tested training tools into the hands of all managers with responsibility for developing people. *Developing Your People* also provides the support needed to use it effectively.

Gower

Evaluating Training

A Resource for Measuring the Results and Impact of Training on People, Departments and Organizations

Sharon Bartram and Brenda Gibson

Training without evaluation is like travelling without a destination. Today's trainers need to demonstrate that what they are doing produces a benefit to the organization that employs them.

Sharon Bartram and Brenda Gibson, authors of the highly successful *Training Needs Analysis*, have turned their attention to the equally important issue of evaluation. They maintain that, by measuring both the results of the learning that takes place and its effect on individuals, departments and organizations, trainers can help people to change their everyday behaviour. And the more you evaluate, the closer you come to creating an environment where learning is a natural part of everyone's routine.

This manual provides a variety of tools and techniques for measuring results. Part One introduces the idea of the evaluation audit. It examines factors such as organizational culture, readiness for learning and evaluation strategy, and shows how to assess current practice and how to plan for the future. Part Two contains 24 instruments for measuring training effectiveness and the impact of training at various levels. They are designed to help you answer two key questions: 'What have people learned?' and 'What difference has their learning made to them, to their department and to the organization?' The forms in Part Two can be copied for immediate use or adapted to suit the needs of your own organization.

Evaluating Training can be used as a means of personal development for trainers; to establish a systematic approach to training evaluation and as a basis for reviewing whatever evaluation you already undertake.

Whether you are new to evaluation or an 'old hand', you will find much to help you here.

Gower

Facilitating Change

Ready-to-Use Training Materials for the Manager

Barry Fletcher

This is a manual designed to help managers to help their staff, using a range of techniques borrowed from the training professional's armoury, with full explanation of how any manager can use them in a team development context. Introductory chapters describe the principles and methods involved in developing people to cope confidently with change. There are questionnaires and suggestions for diagnosing learning needs and recognizing learning opportunities.

At the heart of the manual is a collection of thirtyfive learning activities. Each is self-contained but can be combined with others within the collection to form a more extensive programme of development. All activities start with a brief description and a note of potential benefits, guidance over who it is suitable for and the time and resources required. This is followed by a step-by-step guide to running the activity. Ready-to-copy masters are supplied for any material to be used by participants. The activities are indexed by subject to make it easy for managers to identify the most appropriate for their own needs.

For any manager who'd like to unlock the full potential of his or her team, *Facilitating Change* provides an excellent starting point.

Gower

Flip Chart Games for Trainers

Graham Roberts-Phelps

For many trainers, the flip chart is - and always will be - the simplest and most flexible instant training aid. For any line manager or team leader, working in their new role as trainer and developer, the flip chart may be the only training aid available to them. Hence this collection of *Flip Chart Games for Trainers*.

The 50 exercises, activities and games all revolve around or make active use of a flip chart. In some cases the trainer facilitates the session using the flip chart; in others, it's the participants who use it as part of the exercise. However, whether it's a short icebreaker such as *Jargon Jumble* or *Reasons to Learn*, an energizer such as *Team Talents* or a summarizing exercise such as *Cartoon Time*, or *Jigsaw*, the *Flip Chart Games for Trainers* is certain to engage the imagination and the visual sense of your participants.

Many of the games and exercises can be run in as little as 15 to 25 minutes, making them equally suitable for short meetings or extended training courses. The 'Variations' section helps you to create multiple applications for the exercises or, if you wish, develop them into a longer training activity.

The flip chart is the essential tool for trainers and facilitators and *Flip Chart Games for Trainers* is likely to become as necessary a training aid as the flip charts themselves. A great collection for anyone wishing to inject fun, increase learning and encourage involvement in any session that they run.

Gower

Outdoor Games for Trainers

Carmine Consalvo

Games are perennially popular as a training method for developing teamworking and problem-solving skills. Consalvo has collected together 63 games specifically designed for outdoor use. All of the events can be conducted easily and safely with the minimum of materials and preparation. Many of them can be run equally well indoors.

Each activity is presented in a standard format that includes a summary, a statement of objectives, a note of any materials required, approximate timings and detailed guidance on what to do, when and how, covering both content and process. The exercises vary in length from a few minutes to over an hour. Titles reflect their inventiveness, ranging from: *Space Escape* to *Shuffling the Deck*, and from *Wet Dog Wiggle* to *Ostrich Eggs*. Together they provide a rich store of adventure, energy and memorable learning.

Gower

Pen and Paper Games for Training

Lucy Seifert

Every picture tells a story, a cliché as true in the training room as it is in the news. Pictures, graphics, drawing and writing are key elements in the way that we communicate with each other, process information and learn. Original cartoons, clip art, competitions and conundrums are some of the means used to offer an enjoyable and productive experience for trainer and trainee in *Pen and Paper Games for Training*. Lucy Seifert's eclectic treasury of games and activities illustrates how pen and paper and flipchart paper are all valuable tools for learning. Looking at learning in often unexpected ways, and appealing to all five senses, the games challenge both the logical left- and inspirational right-side of the brain.

Use the games and variations with trainees to relax and involve them, diffusing concerns and anxieties; develop their visual, auditory, linguistic, interpersonal and intrapersonal intelligences; engage diverse personalities - hostile, quiet, shy, serious, anxious, talkative and keen; help them see beyond the mindsets they have at work; bring challenge, co-operation and teamwork into the group dynamic; simplify complex ideas, theories and skills; engage people - and their thought processes - using all of their senses; create an explosion of ideas, impart skills, solve problems and give feedback; assess their knowledge and development; sustain their attention, even in the most repetitive of training tasks such as introductions, expectations and debriefing; and have fun without flippancy.

The author has tested these games in a wide range of group training and one-to-one coaching, including assertiveness, customer care, public speaking and working across cultures. Some cover core elements such as in-depth problem solving; others are fast adrenaline-raisers. At a cursory glance some appear light, but this lightness provides the very tool to dig deeper, to explore and confront complex emotions and issues. Easy to set up, use and explain, undemanding on resources and technology, these games are instantly accessible, rarely needing more than pen and paper, flipchart and markers, handouts and sometimes a treat or prize. Use them in their entirety, adapt a part or a technique to your training topic or environment. These games engage both trainer and trainee by putting the fun into learning.

Gower